RATTLESNAKES

RATTLESNAKES

SANDRA LEE

THE CHILD'S WORLD

PHOTO RESEARCH

Charles Rotter/Gary Lopez Productions

PHOTO CREDITS

Robert and Linda Mitchell: front cover, 24

Joe McDonald: back cover, 6, 9, 10, 31

W. Perry Conway: 2, 14, 16-17, 23, 27

Jeff Foott: 13

Leonard Rue III: 18, 20

Zoological Society of San Diego: 28

Distributed to schools and libraries in the United States by
ENCYCLOPAEDIA BRITANNICA EDUCATIONAL CORP.
310 South Michigan Avenue
Chicago, Illinois 60604

Library of Congress Cataloging-in-Publication Data

Lee, Sandra.

Rattlesnakes / by Sandra Lee.

p.   cm.

Summary: Introduces the physical and behavioral
characteristics of rattlesnakes.

ISBN 0-89565-842-9

1. Rattlesnakes--Juvenile literature.

[1. Rattlesnakes.	2. Snakes.]	I. Title.
QL666.O69L44 1992		91-41153
597.96--dc20		CIP
		AC

For Samantha

When asked to name a favorite animal, not many people would choose the rattlesnake. Most people view rattlesnakes with a mixture of fear and curiosity. If one can get beyond the fear, a beautiful and interesting creature can be found.

There are more than 30 different kinds of rattlesnakes. They are found throughout much of North America. Most rattlesnakes live in the southern United States and Mexico.

A rattlesnake is any snake that has a rattle on the end of its tail. The rattle is a set of bony pieces loosely joined together. The snake uses the rattle to warn people and other animals to stay away. It holds up its tail and shakes the rattle very, very fast. The rattle makes a loud buzzing or hissing sound.

Like other snakes, rattlesnakes are very flexible. A rattlesnake can easily bend itself into a coil. It may sit like this for hours, waiting for something to come along to eat. Rattlesnakes have long backbones that run down the center of their backs. The backbone contains up to 300 bones. It has many joints so the snake can bend easily.

Rattlesnakes have three layers of skin. The tough, outer layer is clear. This skin protects the snake from cuts and scrapes. It covers the snake's whole body—even its eyes.

Snakes grow as long as they live. Sometimes a rattle-snake needs a bigger skin, just as a growing child needs bigger clothes. About twice a year the snake's outer layer of skin becomes dry, white, and crusty. Because this skin covers the snake's eyes, the rattler becomes blind. Fortunately, the worn-out skin soon begins to peel away. Underneath, a new layer of skin has already formed. The snake looks like new!

A rattlesnake's middle layer of skin is thick and folded. These folds are called *scales*. The tough, hard scales overlap and protect the snake's body from bumps and bruises. The broad scales on its underside, called *scutes*, act as little shovels. They dig into the ground to help the snake scoot along.

Not all rattlesnakes use their scutes to slither straight ahead. The sidewinder is a type of rattlesnake that lives in the desert. It gets its name by the way it moves sideways over the sand.

A rattlesnake's bottom layer of skin is the thickest. It also contains the color of the snake's skin. Rattlesnakes are decorated in many different patterns and colors. They are often named after the patterns that appear on their skin. This eastern diamondback has yellow-edged diamond shapes down its back. This type of rattlesnake is the largest. It can grow to over seven feet long.

Rattlesnakes belong to a group of snakes called *pit vipers*. They have small openings, called *pits*, between their eyes and nostrils. The pits can feel heat from the bodies of warm-blooded animals. Rattlesnakes use this sense of heat to hunt for food. They move their heads from side to side to locate the warmest spot. In this way, a rattlesnake can find its prey even in complete darkness.

Rattlesnakes also have large eyes that help them see in dim light. However, they cannot see for very long distances. Snakes do not have eyelids, so their eyes are always open—even when they sleep!

Rattlesnakes do not have ears that are visible like a person's. Their ears are hidden inside their heads. In order to hear, a rattlesnake places its head on the ground. Any animal or person moving nearby causes the ground to vibrate. The snake's jawbone carries the vibrations to its ear.

Rattlesnakes have nostrils, but they also use their tongues to smell. A rattlesnake's tongue flicks out of its mouth to pick up smells from the air.

All rattlesnakes are poisonous. Their poison is a form of saliva called *venom*. A rattlesnake uses its venom only to catch food or to defend itself. The venom is injected into prey through two sharp, hollow teeth called *fangs*. The long fangs fold back when the snake closes its mouth.

Rattlesnakes prefer to dine on small rodents, such as mice, rats, and gophers. They also feed on lizards, frogs, and birds. When a rattler finds something to eat, it thrusts its head forward, almost in a blur. It may strike without rattling or coiling. After injecting its venom, the snake pulls out its fangs and waits. It may look like the animal is escaping, but it doesn't get very far before it dies. Snakes do not have any teeth with which to chew, so they swallow their prey whole. It may take a rattlesnake hours to swallow a large meal!

Baby rattlesnakes do not hatch from eggs like other snakes. They are born alive. Usually there are 10 to 20 babies in a litter. The size of the litter depends on the size of the mother. A large female can have as many as 60 babies at a time! However, only a few of the baby rattlesnakes survive their first year. Many die from excessive cold or heat, or from starvation.

Rattlesnakes can be dangerous, but there is no reason to be overly fearful. Being careful is the important thing to remember. If you are hiking where there are rattlesnakes, wear sturdy hiking boots and thick coverings on your lower legs. Rattlesnakes will not bite unless they feel threatened, so don't reach into any rocks or brush where you cannot see. If you see a rattlesnake, keep your distance and respect this fascinating creature.

THE CHILD'S WORLD
NATUREBOOKS

Wildlife Library

Space Library

Adventure Library